D1551216

What Happens When
Wheels
Turn?

What Happens When

Wheels Turn?

Daphne Butler

RSVP

RAINTREE
STECK-VAUGHN
P U B L I S H E R S
The Steck-Vaughn Company

Austin, Texas

© Copyright 1996, text, Steck-Vaughn Company

Published by Raintree Steck-Vaughn Publishers, an imprint of Steck-Vaughn Company

Library of Congress Cataloging-in-Publication Data

Butler, Daphne, 1945–
      What happens when wheels turn? / Daphne Butler.
            p.   cm. — (What happens when—?)
      Includes index.
      ISBN 0-8172-4152-3
      1. Wheels—Juvenile literature. [1. Wheels.]   I. Title.
      II. Series: Butler, Daphne, 1945–   What happens when—?
      TJ181.5.B88   1996
      621.8'11—dc20   95-11782
                                                                            CIP
                                                                             AC

Printed and bound in Singapore
1 2 3 4 5 6 7 8 9 0 99 98 97 96 95

Contents

A New Technology

More than 5,000 years ago, people discovered a new **technology**. It changed their lives.

The idea probably came from the use of trunks of small trees as rollers.

Before long, people invented carts with wheels. These carts could carry a person's goods and belongings.

Changing Wheels

Over the years, people improved the technology.

They gave wheels **spokes** to make them lighter. Iron rims were added to make them stronger.

Today, wheels have strong metal **hubs** and thick rubber tires filled with air. They can travel very quickly.

More Wheels

Wheels are used in many ways.

They are used as paddles to drive boats in water. They are also used to lift helicopters in the air.

Wheels are used in other vehicles, too. Can you name some?

Not Just Transportation

Wheels provide a lot of fun!

What other wheels can you think of that help you have a good time?

Can wheels be dangerous?

A quickly spinning wheel with sharp
teeth cuts easily through pieces of
wood. It is called a **circular saw**, and
it makes a terrible noise.

The teeth are kept very sharp by
using a special tool.

15

Grinding Wheels

Grinding wheels are made of hard stone. They spin around quickly.

Objects that touch them are made smooth. Sometimes liquid is used to wash away the **grit**.

Freshly made paper is wound onto large rollers.

Toilet paper is wound onto small cardboard rollers. This way you can pull it off one sheet at a time.

Newspaper is wound onto huge rollers that fit printing machines. When the wheels turn, newspapers are printed, cut, and folded.

This machine is weaving red cloth.
At the back of it, you can see where
the thread comes from.

Without wheels, reels, and rollers,
it could not work at all.

21

Cog Wheels

Inside an old-fashioned watch or clock, there are many wheels with teeth around the edge. The teeth fit together so that when one wheel turns, they all turn. These are cog wheels.

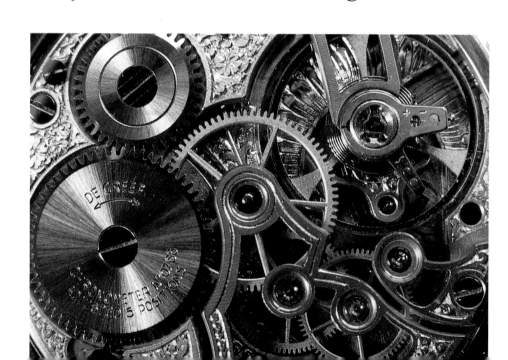

When cog wheels are different sizes,
the smaller ones must move faster
to keep up with the bigger ones.
Can you see why?

Cog wheels are an important part
of many machines.

Pumping Water

This machine uses cog wheels to pump water out of a well.

The animal turns one cog wheel as it walks around and around. This turns another cog wheel, which joins to the wheel with the jars.

The jars lift water out of the well. They tip it into a ditch.

Powerful Wheels

Waterwheels called **turbines** make electricity. When water or steam rushes past the turbine blades, they spin around. The blades turn a motor that makes the electricity.

turbine blades

What would your life be like without wheels or electricity?

circular saw A saw with a round cutting blade that has teeth

conveyor belt A belt running on rollers. It moves things from one place to another.

grit Tiny rough particles of sand or stone

hub The central part of a wheel

28

pulley A wheel with rope around it. It is used for lifting heavy things.

spokes Wires that are inside the hub of a wheel

technology The application of knowledge

turbine A kind of engine with a wheel inside it. The wheel is turned by gas, water, or steam.

29

Index

Globe Enterprises © 1993
Published in association with Macdonald Young Books Ltd